TARGETED LEADERSHIP
BUILDING A TEAM THAT HITS THE MARK

By Tracey Ballas and Christopher Novak

Credits

Editing: Erika Konowalow

Cover and book design: Key Metts

ISBN: 0-917505-22-0

ISBN-13: 978-0-917505-22-5

1. Leadership 2. Early Childhood 3. After School 4. Collaboration
5. Education

c. 2010 Tracey Ballas, Christopher Novak. All rights reserved

Published by School-Age NOTES, P.O. Box 476, New Albany, OH 43054

Printed in Canada

DEDICATION

To four very special men in my life:
Todd, Justin, Ethan and Dylan.
I have watched you take risks, challenge yourselves,
try new things and to see it through
when times were tough.
You were my inspiration to do the same.
Thank you!

To Daddy and in memory of Mom,
with love and appreciation for exemplifying leadership
at home, at work, and in our community.
Your influence has left an indelible mark on my life.

— **Tracey Ballas**

TABLE OF CONTENTS

FOREWORD

There are after-school programs all over the country that you know are special the moment you walk into them. They are exceptional not just because of their resources, facility or unique program content, but rather because of the people in them who give off extraordinary professional vibes. These programs have leaders who cultivate greatness in others. Kids everywhere excel in programs like these.

The best advice I could give to anyone wanting to develop a stimulating, high-quality after-school program would be to hire good people. But even when you do hire well, every program leader must focus on motivating, inspiring and training her staff members to achieve a consistent, top-notch performance that radiates that aura of greatness. This book is full of ideas, advice and practical tips that will help you do just that.

Tracey Ballas and Christopher Novak share years of experience working with after-school programs, training leaders, presenting workshops, teaching classes and reviewing the best resources available for after-school professionals. And this book is one such resource. You will want it as part of your professional library. Read it, learn from it, enjoy it and refer back to it often as a reference to support your work. The authors are experts in their fields and the wisdom they share in these pages will help us all no matter where we are in our careers. This book is part of my library and I highly recommend that you include it in yours.

— **Paul G. Young, Ph.D.**
Interim Chief Executive, National AfterSchool Association and
Past President, National Association of Elementary School Principals

PREFACE

Leaders are not born, they are cultivated. I am proof of that!

After college, where I studied elementary education and child psychology, I got a job with a rural school district that had received a small grant to establish their first after-school program. Having never worked in or visited an after-school program put me at a distinct disadvantage. However, I accepted the position as the director with enthusiasm and determination, and went on to implement a program for 30 children with two volunteer staff members. Soon after, I opened a second site for the school district. Although I looked feverishly through my textbooks and class notes from college, I found little guidance to give me assurance that I was doing everything the right way.

A few years later I became the director of child-care services for a large metropolitan YMCA, where I had 20 after-school programs serving nearly 1,000 children and was managing more than 100 staff members spread across five school districts. I was 26 years old and nothing in my education had equipped me for the enormous leadership role I suddenly found myself taking on.

I hungered for opportunities to network with leaders and mentors and was ravenous for training and professional development. I also had a strong desire to advocate for children and families. I looked for state and national organizations to join, but found nothing. Instead, I found that countless people across the country were on the same journey to develop quality after-school programs and an infrastructure to support after-school professionals. I also realized that they felt the same need for resources, information and support.

In the midst of this void and with a united vision, a group of us established a national organization, the National AfterSchool Association, and many statewide affiliates, such as the Ohio After-School Association. These organizations provide conferences and training, networking opportunities and professional development, and public policy and advocacy opportunities to thousands in the after-school field throughout the United States.

To my surprise, in my late 20s, I found myself president of both of these organizations. Once again, my education had not formally prepared me for this leadership role. I found myself taking risks and developing skills out of necessity. I was fortunate to be surrounded by newfound colleagues who modeled passion, energy, vision, persistence, creativity and resourcefulness. In other words, they exemplified true leadership!

I realize with certainty that the early-childhood and after-school fields have come a long way in the past 25 years. Yet we are still hungry for resources and information that can strengthen our programs and staff members. I am equally certain that my leadership was not born within me, but rather cultivated and honed through the careful guidance of supervisors, colleagues and mentors showing me the way.

Christopher Novak, a human resources professional for more than 20 years, has joined me to write this book that we believe will hit the mark in providing the information, support and guidance to early-childhood and after-school professionals who are honing their own leadership skills and cultivating the next generation of leaders. We also offer information on how to build a well-balanced team that can take the program's potential to a new level of success. It is designed to be a practical go-to resource that is on target with tips and worksheets that can be put into practice immediately and repeatedly. It is filled with, we hope, inspirational stories and information that will linger in you mind long after the book is closed.

In following a writing style established by the Center for the Child Care Workforce, please note that we generally use the female pronouns when referring to staff or team members because of the large preponderance of women in the early childhood and after-school workforce, and because it becomes awkward to repeat *he/she* and *his/her*. But we would also like to recognize the importance of men working in the field, and hope that men and women will feel included and valued as they use this resource.

— **Tracey Ballas**
January 2010

INTRODUCTION

Leaders in the early-childhood and after-school field face a difficult challenge in having to build a quality, child-centered learning experience staffed with motivated and talented professionals within the confines of limited resources, variable support and, often, inadequate space. It is a challenge that many meet with surprising success, buoyed by the strength, resourcefulness and persistence of effective internal leadership.

Indeed, given the factors that influence the outcome of any early-childhood or after-school program, two emerge as the foundation of top programs. The first is that model programs are led by solid leadership at the top; program directors whose own leadership philosophies include continual growth. The second is that the best programs are supported by a well-balanced team of professionals whose collective talents and energy are well-matched, diverse and committed to their profession.

A team is composed of a leader and a group of followers who are engaged in activities that have purpose, direction and content. Each of the team members offers the group skills and traits; and it is identifying, cultivating and balancing those skills and traits across the entire team that determines in large measure how effective the team will be in achieving its goals.

Skills are substance while traits are essence. Skills are often tangible, visible and readily identifiable and can be taught or learned over time with practice and training. They are the mechanics — the how-to for any task or responsibility — and can be objectively evaluated.

Traits tend to be innate — you have them or you don't. They are not easily acquired and are difficult to enhance. Traits are an expression of a person's core characteristics and as such can be open to interpretation and subjective analysis. They can take years to shape or reshape and while conjuring or altering a trait is not impossible it is nonetheless daunting because it involves reprogramming core behaviors.

Building a team that hits the mark every time comes down to creating harmony between what can be mastered (skills) and what can be mustered (traits).

ZEN AND ARCHERY

In Japan, archery is woven tightly into the national heritage, transcending the mere physical effort required to place a projectile at the center of a target by means of controlled tension. Archery in Japan is an art with deep Zen roots that blends the bodily exercises of movement with mental, emotional and even spiritual focus to aim not at a target but at a deeper understanding of self. It is an extraordinary balance of substance and essence — of skills and traits.

The skills required to perform the task involve gripping the bow, notching an arrow, drawing the string, sighting the target line, cleanly releasing the fingers and so forth. These are demonstrations of muscle-controlled actions that are necessary to perform the task of releasing an arrow from a bow. All of these skills can be taught, observed, evaluated and improved with practice.

Skills lend themselves well to a traditional teacher-student experience where a transfer of knowledge can be measured, tested and reinforced. They tend to be specific in nature or serve a particular purpose. Skills also can be absent in the student and yet developed in a relatively brief period of time through demonstration and a repetitive curriculum.

By contrast, the traits to master this ancient craft include discipline, patience, focus, calm, reflection, connection and balance. On what scale do you measure reflection? By what standard do you determine discipline? The traditional metric of evaluation escapes us when we consider these elements of truly mastering archery. It is not that one cannot improve their level of patience, for example, but that to do so requires significant time, unique circumstances and special guidance.

Traits are expressions of our inner self and that makes them applicable across the spectrum of our daily existence. If we are undisciplined in learning archery it is reasonable to assume we are undisciplined in other aspects of our life because that characteristic is part of who we are.

The best skills without the right traits produce an archer who is inconsistent — hitting the target some of the time but without predictability and confidence. The best traits without skills produce an archer with good intentions but poor aim — a dangerous proposition if you are downrange. Skills and traits must be in balance — in harmony — to produce an archer whose results are always as intended.

The same requirement to forge a balanced relationship between skills and traits forms the basis of any leader's search for excellence in evaluating the capabilities and potential of current (and future) staff members. The successful program director will look closely at not only the tangible skill sets that colleagues bring to the team but also their individual traits, as these reveal insight on strengths and weaknesses and suggests how a leader can best deploy her team.

Placing a priority on balancing skills and traits also helps the leader to make accurate hiring decisions. It is easy to be impressed with skills portrayed on a well-prepared resume but placing an overemphasis on those abilities can trap a leader into missing glaring gaps in critical traits. Similarly, a candidate's superb traits in areas such as charm, charisma, energy, enthusiasm and personality can often mask deficiencies in necessary skill sets. Being swayed by a candidate based only on the apparent personal chemistry they produce is a mistake that can leave your team lacking in the skills to do the job right.

Teaching you how to create a balance between skills and traits —— to establish a harmony of substance and essence; to synergize what can be mastered with what can be mustered — is the bull's-eye at which this book aims. It is a lesson that successful leaders in almost any field have learned: Balance is the secret to creating a high-performing team of professionals who are able and willing to hit the mark every time.

THE CONDUCTOR, THE CONNECTOR AND THE CRUISE DIRECTOR

Cultivating harmony across the entire team between what can be mastered and what must be mustered is the secret to achieving exceptional performance. Thus, it would be beneficial to create a language where core elements of that balance could be easily communicated. The goal of that language is to define the expression of skills and traits in terms that we can relate to so that we can then discuss, train, evaluate, discern and examine our program in a bold, new way.

In the same fashion that Myers-Briggs gave us a language to understand personality or that Hersey and Blanchard gave us a framework to view stale leadership norms with a fresh perspective, our custom-tailored language allows us to visualize what the elements of balance look like in the early-childhood or after-school workplace.

The Conductor

Keeping the program on track is a well-organized, detail-oriented Conductor. This team member is mindful of regulations, policy, procedures, compliance, schedules and all necessary program-planning documents. Generally, she is neat, orderly and has excellent follow-through with parents and program or school leaders. Conductors are reliable colleagues who are skilled at program and time management. Terms that describe such team members include:

organized	detail-oriented
prompt	computer literate
good writer	accounting background
good follow-through	punctual
neat	orderly
careful	well-prepared
has a plan B	reliable
multitask-oriented	flexible
safety-conscience	a problem-solver
efficient	diligent

aware of the rules, regulations and procedures

The Connector

Building relationships is at the heart of every Connector. These are the team members who are skilled at reaching out to children, parents, program or school leaders and colleagues to establish positive relationships. Connectors have a high emotional intelligence that enhances their ability to identify with a child's emotional needs, compliment the janitor or bond with a parent. They are comfortable in situations that require sensitivity, empathetic listening or compassionate communication while respecting confidentiality and privacy. Terms that describe such team members include:

nurturing	loving
kind	caring
child-centered	warm
compassionate	friendly
sociable	collaborator
gentle	good listener
amicable	good communicator
people-oriented	good networker
positive attitude	considerate
empathetic	sympathetic
big-hearted	concerned
patient	team player
relationship builder	

The Cruise Director

High energy and resourcefulness are the hallmarks of every Cruise Director. These are the team members who are talented at keeping the children engaged in meaningful activities that are often creative, active or just plain fun. Cruise Directors are often popular with the children because they cultivate opportunities for learning and doing that can take the form of clubs, athletics, homework, music, arts or computer skills. Terms that describe such team members include:

fun	resourceful
vibrant	creative
energetic	artistic
playful	active
musical	athletic
imaginative	ingenious
multitask-oriented	organized
well-prepared	flexible
charismatic	outgoing
inventive	lively
good planner	optimistic
innovative	vital
enthusiastic	dynamic

Core Characteristics

Common to all our team members should be skills and traits that contribute to a well-run, professional program. Essential elements of any good team and that are central to constructive collaboration among staff members include being:

flexible	professional
a problem-solver	punctual
reliable	self-motivated
energetic	responsible
tolerant	a team player
honest	trustworthy
accountable	self-aware
a good communicator	ethical
mature	proactive
open-minded	friendly
eager	observant

principled, dedicated, committed and fair

Other important skills and traits include showing initiative; showing common sense; modeling good hygiene; modeling a positive attitude; coming to work for more than the paycheck; having an appropriate sense of humor; and possessing experience.

PUTTING THE PUZZLE TOGETHER

Is it possible for any one candidate to embody all of the skills and traits that are listed? Not likely. Yet, as you review these skills and traits, which ones can the children do without? Which ones do you not want a colleague to possess? This may be asking too much of any one staff member, but not too much from an entire team.

Like a puzzle, when you begin you just lay out the pieces. If you step back and assess the pieces you can often see the shapes and colors that will likely fit together. Filling in the gaps requires patience and strategy. You use the picture on the box top to keep you focused on the desired outcome. Piece by piece you put the puzzle together and at last create a complete and pretty picture.

You need to be just as strategic when you assess the strengths and weaknesses of your current staff members. You need to be able to clearly visualize the gaps you want to fill, as well as the overlap you want to avoid. Those are the shapes and colors. You need to be able to articulate that vision in your recruitment, sourcing and interviewing efforts and never lose sight of the complete picture you are trying to put together. If done with care and intent, you can piece together a pretty picture of a balanced staff.

So what does a program look like when it is out of balance? If you have Conductors and Connectors but no Cruise Directors, it looks like a program that is dull, boring and low on energy. It may be lacking in games, sports, artist creativity or inventive exploration. Without the Cruise Director, program planning and resourceful ideas are often harder to come by.

If you have Connectors and Cruise Directors but no Conductors, the program is likely to look disorganized and chaotic. Projects can go uncompleted, paperwork gets lost in the shuffle and cabinets can be in disarray. Who is ready with another plan when things don't go as scheduled? Who will be unflappable when the licensing inspector shows up for a surprise visit or the grant application is due? Without a detail-oriented Conductor, follow-through may be lax.

If you have Cruise Directors and Conductors but no Connectors then the program can appear less welcoming and cold. After all, Connectors recognize that a colleague or parent left yesterday with a smile but walked in today with a frown. They will be a sympathetic listener and help process feelings and empower problem solving. They model collaboration with parents, teachers and program or school leaders. They are the custodian's favorite staff member.

But to have a picture-perfect staff requires that some qualities are necessary for all staff members to exhibit, such as common sense, reliability, professionalism, a sense of humor, flexibility, dedication and personal initiative.

Creating a Balanced Staff

Conductor + Connector − Cruise Director
= A boring, dull program

Connector + Cruise Director − Conductor
= A disorganized, chaotic program

Cruise Director + Conductor − Connector
= A program that lacks warmth and nurturing

Conductor + Connector + Cruise Director = **BALANCE**

➤ For a poster of this formula, see the CD-ROM included with this book.

FILLING THE GAPS

After carefully assessing the skills and traits that you have or lack in your current staff members you can then decide what else you need to create a balanced team. It will be different each time.

For instance, if your team is perfectly balanced but your Cruise Director is leaving to take another job, then you need to find another Cruise Director to remain in balance. However, while this last Cruise Director was very artistic, she never cleaned up well after stirring the children into a creative frenzy. So this time, develop a want ad that not only describes an artistic wonder but sprinkles in words such as organized, neat or orderly.

➤ For a starter set of Terms of Endearment, see Page 73. A printable version can be found on the CD-ROM included with this book.

Or if you realize that your team is overrun with Connectors, then see the bright side when one of them tells you they are leaving. This provides you with the perfect opportunity to realign the team and intentionally create balance. Decide if you need a Conductor or Cruise Director or a combination of both. Use your list of descriptors, also known as Terms of Endearment, and create an ad that paints a portrait of the kind of candidate you want to attract. Ask for what you and your program truly need each and every time you write an ad.

This list is not stagnant. It is meant to be a resource that evolves over time. While reading or listening to conversations, pick out words that articulate qualities that you want to elicit and add them to the list. You may even notice that there are buzzwords that are ideal today but over time are less meaningful. Update the list of descriptors to reflect changes in the field or advancing needs of your team and program.

Following are some sample ads for each position. However, it is important that you craft an ad specifying exactly what you and your program need at the time of your search for a new team member. Be very intentional with each word you select from your list of descriptors to create the ad. Each ad will be as unique as the person you are seeking to fill your position. Remember, this is your chance to strengthen any weaknesses and fill in the skills and traits that are missing in your program. The strategic selection of words will affect the kind of candidate you attract from this ad.

CONDUCTOR, CONNECTOR, CRUISE DIRECTOR

Sample Ads

FOR A CONDUCTOR

Wanted: Detail-oriented professional to work with school-age children and families. Comfortable as a solution finder, organizer and with taking initiative. Models flexibility, humor, teamwork and follow-through.

FOR A CONNECTOR

Wanted: Caring, articulate, early-childhood professional who is experienced with young children. High energy problem-solver who models collaboration and compassion with adults and children.

FOR A CRUISE DIRECTOR

Wanted: Energetic, knowledgeable recreation specialist who enjoys school-age children and their families. Resourceful, creative planner who can multitask with ease. Hands-on and inventive while mature and responsible.

Notice that these ads look very different than the average ones you find in a newspaper, on a Web site or a bulletin board. That's good! The idea is to stand out from the crowd. Don't be surprised if you receive fewer responses to such ads. That's good, as well. You want people to resonate with each word as if the ad was written just for them or know by the ad's requirements that the job is not for them. This helps you get closer to exactly the kind of candidate that you are seeking and helps not to waste your time with those who don't meet your current needs. Generic ads will attract mediocre candidates. Children and their families expect and deserve so much more than that. And, as a member of the team, we do too.

➤ See Page 74 for additional ideas for where to look for staff members and volunteers. A printable version can be found on the CD-ROM included with this book.

Word of mouth is a powerful and effective method of finding new staff members. Print your uniquely worded want ad on colorful paper so it will get noticed and take copies of it with you everywhere you go. Whether you are going to the grocery store, professional meetings or trainings, workout facility, community or volunteer events, salon or barbershop, car wash, drugstore, library, gas station, neighborhood cookout, sporting event or other common places in your world, take this ad with you. Talk to people about your opening everywhere you go and give them the ad so they know very specifically the type of person you are looking for at this time. Make sure that every parent and current staff member in your program has a copy, as well. Both groups have a vested interest in seeing that you hire a good person for this position.

CONDUCTOR, CONNECTOR, CRUISE DIRECTOR

THE EMPLOYMENT LIFE CYCLE

Leadership in any organization is a multifaceted challenge. Understanding a few constants in the shifting landscape can be the difference between success and failure. One of those constants is the employment life cycle.

Quite simply, the employment life cycle (or ELC) is a way to describe the recurring pattern of activity that leaders engage in as they move a program, team or organization forward. The ELC describes the process for selecting staff members and developing their leadership skills.

Devoting the necessary time and energy to this process should dominate the leader's responsibilities, just as program planning should dominate the responsibilities of her staff members. The ELC highlights areas where leaders should invest their time, resources and efforts to build strong, vibrant programs that exceed parental expectations and provide the quality learning experience that children deserve.

The ELC is not a stagnant marker. It is a dynamic interaction of people and processes that acknowledges the almost biological nature of any organization. Programs are constantly in motion: changing, developing, evolving, adapting and growing in response to internal and external stimuli. The ELC flows from this reality and gives the leader an opportunity to see the enormous task of creating and sustaining an excellence-based program in smaller, more manageable pieces. The employment life cycle is built around five components: assessment, recruitment, orientation, coaching and termination.

There is a logical current to this cycle that invites leaders to pursue an almost sequential or linear progression that also makes good common sense. Recognizing this natural order gives the leader a road map to follow in building a highly effective team of professionals capable of producing an exceptional program for children.

Assessment

Every journey worth taking has a clear, unmistakable beginning point from which progress is measured. "Assessment" is that starting point for the ELC. This is the process of organizational introspection. It is the hard look in the mirror that provides an accurate reflection of the current state of the program and the people in it.

Assessment is about identifying the specific strengths and weaknesses of your team. It's about seeing how the pieces fit together; how they function and, more important, why they function in the manner that they do. What is it about each of your colleagues that adds to or subtracts from the overall quality learning experience that you are creating for the children? What runs very well in the program and what is broken? Where are relationships strong and who is responsible for building those bonds?

Assessment does more than gather information. It applies that knowledge. Leaders take the assessment results and develop an analysis that aligns the program's goals and responsibilities with the skills and traits of its staff members, then uses those comparisons to identify deficiencies that need to be addressed. A good analysis will show areas of overlapping strength as well as areas where no (or inadequate) proficiency exists.

An important aspect of assessment is remembering the difference between skills and traits. As stated earlier, this comes down to understanding one simple concept — knowing what can be mastered and what can be mustered. Skills can be mastered, traits can be mustered. Placing a priority on balancing skills and traits also helps the leader to make accurate assessments when considering key hiring decisions.

Recruitment

The second element of the ELC encompasses the search for professional talent and the process of selecting and hiring that talent. "Recruitment" is a science wrapped in an art so an effective leader must be proficient in both aspects of the process.

There are three stages to recruitment: sourcing, interviewing and the hiring decision.

SOURCING

Sourcing is identifying a pool of qualified and motivated candidates who can meet your needs. It is reaching out to the best channels available to share the news of your career opportunity with people who are qualified for and may be interested in the position. The number of options available to broadcast your opening has exploded in recent years. Not long ago, a job opening would have appeared in the classifieds section of the local newspaper or possibly in a printed school newsletter or community publication. Today, in addition to those outlets, the Internet has created countless opportunities to advertise a job vacancy.

Online job boards such as Monster.com, HotJobs.com and CareerBuilder.com are staples in the recruitment process because they bring together employers and candidates. These job boards list virtually every career and post openings from virtually any organization on a global basis. Candidates type in filtering criteria about the kind of job they are seeking, location, salary, etc., to whittle down the massive volume of data to a manageable size.

Word of mouth remains one of the most successful methods for finding qualified candidates, so in the course of advertising in print and online media do not overlook the value of sharing news of your job vacancy in conversations with other people. By making people in your network of colleagues, friends, neighbors and congregation aware of the opening, you draw in the network of each of those people as well and the pool of potential candidates widens quickly.

INTERVIEWING: THE TELEPHONE SCREEN

The second phase of the recruitment process is to evaluate the skills and traits of the candidates through interviewing. The first interviews are generally conducted by phone and amount to an initial screening.

It's important to contact the candidates whose resumes merit additional exploration and schedule each person for a preliminary phone interview. The telephone interview should take between 15 and 30 minutes and is your first opportunity to learn more about the candidate's background, motivations and potential. Make certain that you will not be interrupted during the call and that you have the individual's resume (and/or application) and cover letter with you. You should also have a set of questions that you want to get through. These are similar for every candidate and typically ask the person to expand on information they've presented in their resume or application.

The telephone screen also allows you to pre-sell your program by sharing exciting elements of the position and increasing a candidate's interest in joining your team. Opening the call with a brief introduction that includes your background, program highlights and an overview of the position gives the candidate some context in which to answer your questions.

> A sample set of telephone screening questions is provided on Page 76. A printable version can be found on the CD-ROM included with this book.

One of the advantages of conducting a telephone screening is the ability to assess some of the intangible elements of a candidacy that cannot be extracted from a resume or application. How articulate is the candidate? How readily can they respond to your questions and how coherent and relevant are the answers? Can they expand on the experience and skills presented on their resume? What is their enthusiasm level for the position and why do they see this as an opportunity for them? Opening the screening up at the end to allow the candidate to ask questions also can provide the interviewer with valuable information based on the nature of the candidate's inquiries.

It is important to take careful notes during the telephone screening, noting not only their answers but also recording your overall satisfaction with the candidate's responses. A numeric scale of 1 to 10 might be helpful in gauging the thoroughness or appropriateness of a candidate's dialogue so that you can compare your satisfaction levels of candidates.

Once you have completed all of the telephone screenings, review the results and sort the candidates from strongest to weakest and look for a natural cutoff point where the results take a dramatic dip. There is no magic number of candidates that you should screen to create an on-site interview pool. The number will depend on the number of resumes received, the strength (on paper) of those candidates and the time you have to devote to this phase. However, it would not be unreasonable to plan on screening by phone a dozen candidates with the goal of identifying the top three to five for face-to-face interviews.

Take comfort in knowing that you do not have to interview every candidate who responds to your posting. You are free to request interviews with only the applicants whose resumes list the skills, training and experience that make them the best candidates for the job. However, you cannot rule out an applicant for an interview because of race, color, religion, political affiliation, national origin, disability, marital status, gender or age.

With the pool now narrowed to whom you want to interview, establish a tentative schedule for those face-to-face sessions. Be sure to coordinate with any other staff members whom you are including in the interview process to ensure that they are available. Then, call each of the top candidates from the phone-screening phase and invite them for an interview at one of the selected dates and times. Ask them to allow approximately 90 minutes for this meeting. Send them a written confirmation of the interview along with directions to your location, reporting-in procedures and any literature or information about the program that would be appropriate.

INTERVIEWING: ON-SITE MEETING

Recruitment is one of the most exciting elements of any leader's responsibilities because it is a rare opportunity to increase the quality and potential of your program in one decision. You are searching for talent that will elevate your team and accelerate the continuous improvement that every program leader strives to achieve for the children they serve. There is no step in the recruitment process more crucial to selecting the right person than the face-to-face interview. It is the make-or-break moment where you can most accurately gauge the totality of a candidate and assess how she would fit with your needs.

Give this phase the time, attention and commitment that it deserves. There is an old adage in human resources that says, "Higher tough, manage easy," meaning quite simply that the tougher you are on the front-end in selecting the best candidate for the position, the easier it will be later when this person is part of your team.

Any vacancy-imposed hardships on a program can burden the team members, but rushing to fill a position can be crippling when that new hire turns out to be a bigger problem than she solves. In the same way that an ideal match can ignite a performance burst within a program, a poor hire can devastate a team and leave the leadership mired in a malaise that is as tragic as it is avoidable. You need to get this decision right.

Devoting time, energy and careful planning in preparation

for interviewing candidates pays off. Interviewing, for any given position, is a process that is replicated with each candidate. Be consistent and organized.

Take steps to ensure that the interviews are as productive as possible. If you interview many candidates, you will need detailed notes to remember each candidate. In addition to having the notes with you that you took during the phone interviews, create a list of questions that you will ask every candidate. Think in detail about the type of questions that will help determine whether the candidate possesses the skills, traits, attributes and experience that you are seeking. Be sure to ask the same questions of every candidate.

Designate a staff member to greet each candidate as she arrives. The greeter plays an important role by providing a welcoming first impression and conveying a sense that the candidate is expected. The greeter will also note the time of arrival to gauge punctuality. Have the greeter show the candidate where to wait, offer something to drink and show her where the staff restroom is located. A nervous candidate will appreciate these creature comforts.

Make sure that the greeter knows if the candidate was requested to bring paperwork with them. The greeter should request this paperwork when she welcomes the candidate and deliver it to you before the interview so that you can look it over and have it available to refer to during the interview. A candidate who brings requested paperwork is demonstrating responsibility and follow-through. Do not ask the candidate to bring a photograph and do not take a photograph of the candidate at any time during the interview process.

Create a conducive atmosphere for the interview. For example, you may want to use two chairs at a round table instead of creating a power imbalance by sitting behind a desk while the candidate sits at a chair on the other side of the desk. If you must interview in a room with a desk, consider using two chairs on the same side of the desk to avoid a sense of intimidation. Make sure to have paper, pencils and drinking water available on the desk or table. If using a round table, consider covering with a tablecloth and placing flowers in the center. This sends a message to the candidate that planning and preparation took place and creating a homey environment is valued.

Be prompt for the interview in order to model the expectation of punctuality. Do not permit interruptions during the interview except for emergencies. Designate a staff member to answer the telephone and intercept potential interruptions.

Be a good listener. Although you have prepared a detailed list of questions in preparation for the interview, remember to listen to the answers carefully.

Maintain good eye contact with the candidate. Be aware of your body language and facial expressions. This communicates so much to a candidate without saying a word. Shake hands with the candidate when you greet her and when you end the interview. Make sure to thank the candidate for taking the time to meet with you.

To avoid violating any federal laws or employment acts, do not ask questions regarding the candidate's age, race, sexual orientation, religion, creed, national origin, marital status, physical impairment or disability. Title I of the Americans with Disabilities Act also prohibits asking questions about hospitalizations, psychological or psychiatric care, prescription medications, absences from work, health-related reasons that may prohibit the candidate from performing the job that they are applying for, and treatment for drug addiction or alcoholism. If you have any questions regarding the legality of a question, consult with a lawyer who specializes in employment law before scheduling your first interview.

Write down the candidates' responses to questions clearly, legibly and accurately. After the interview, you may want to create a grid that lists each candidate, along with the major attributes and job requirements. Judith Lindenberger with the Lindenberger Group recommends rating each candidate on a scale of 1 to 5 for each requirement/attribute. The candidate with the highest rating is probably your best candidate for the job.

The following questions can be an effective addition to any interview and are easily adapted to any level of candidate you are considering. The purpose is twofold. First, the questions illuminate key traits and skills that are desirable in all team members. Second, the questions reveal tendencies toward Conductor, Connector or Cruise Director so as to more accurately assess their fit with the existing team.

The interviewer can gain additional insight into the candidate's skills by asking her to compose a written answer to any of the following questions. This writing sample provides an opportunity to evaluate their thought process, writing skills and level of literacy. Give the candidate the question on a piece of paper as they arrive and let them know they have 10 minutes to complete their answer.

Differentiating between Conductor, Connector and Cruise Director is one of the focal points of the interview process. The more readily a candidate's tendencies in these categories can be identified, the more accurately her overall fit within the program can be determined.

How a candidate prioritizes each set of three words — and the explanation as to why she chose that order — is important information to consider. Present the candidate with one set of words early in the questioning, another set mid-way through the interview and the final set of words near the end of the question period. The following questions are examples of how to word the questions for an interview.

1. **Rank these three words in the order of importance to you as an early-childhood or after-school professional: organized, good communicator and imaginative. Tell me why you answered that way.**

2. **Rank these three words in the order of importance to you as an early-childhood or after-school professional: careful, compassionate and playful. Tell me why you answered that way.**

3. **Rank these three words in the order of importance to you as an early-childhood or after-school professional: policies, relationships and flexibility. Tell me why you answered that way.**

(When creating these questions, be sure to include one characteristic from each category: conductor, connector and cruise director.)

The following questions can help determine how best a candidate will fit in your program. Words in parentheses help identify certain traits that are sought.

WHEN INTERVIEWING FOR A CONDUCTOR

- On a field trip, the bus breaks down and pulls safely to a rest area. What do you do? (crisis-management, common sense)
- What are the three most important rules in an early-childhood or after-school program? (regulation/policy, priorities)
- One of your colleagues is chronically late and there doesn't seem to be any corrective action being taken. Whom do you approach and what do you say? (punctuality)

WHEN INTERVIEWING FOR A CONNECTOR

- You notice one child who is not engaged in any activity or interactions with other children. How would you approach this child? (empathy)
- How do you break up cliques that have formed, leaving some children feeling excluded? (tolerance)
- You notice a colleague who is quieter than usual. Do you approach the colleague and ask what is wrong or do you respect their privacy? (compassion)

WHEN INTERVIEWING FOR A CRUISE DIRECTOR

- The budget is extremely tight and supplies are running low. What do you do? (resourcefulness, imagination)
- The owner of a local Chinese restaurant drops by to donate 100 new take-out boxes and chopsticks. Do you accept the donation and if so what do you do with them? (creativity, spontaneity)
- Describe some of the best activities you have facilitated with children? (child-centered, athletic/artistic)

QUESTIONS THAT HELP IDENTIFY TRAITS

- There is a deep pool of candidates for this position. Why should you be hired over any of the other candidates? (self-assessment, self-esteem, drive, motivation)
- Describe one professional decision that you made that turned out to be a mistake or something you would do differently if you had to do it over. How did you correct it or how would you do it

differently given the chance? (self-criticism, honesty, humility)
- A colleague is beginning to tell you that they heard that the newest employee was hired at a pay rate higher than anyone else on the team. She wants your opinion. How do you react? (ethics, confidentiality)
- How do you differentiate between discipline and punishment? (philosophy, behavior management)
- Tell me what it is about the early-childhood or after-school field that attracts you to this work? (motivation)

QUESTIONS THAT HELP IDENTIFY SKILLS

Consider the following situations and describe how you would react:
- A parent approaches you and says she has something important to discuss regarding her child while simultaneously a pitcher of milk goes crashing to the floor from the snack table and two children break out into a tug-of-war over a popular toy. (multitasking)
- You have been promised the gymnasium space from 4 to 5 p.m., but when you arrive with the children there are 100 chairs set up for a PTA meeting later that evening. It has been raining all day so outdoor play is not an option and the children need to release pent up energy. What do you do? (flexibility)
- The school or organization that hosts your early-childhood or after-school program has had a change in leadership. The new leader is not supportive of using their space for your program. How would you approach the new leader to gain her acceptance and support? (relationship-building)
- Every professional has an emotional limit. How do you recognize when your frustration level at work is reaching its limit and how do you deal with it? (anger management, balance)

Interviewing: Checking References

Once you have reviewed the resumes and writing samples and interviewed all candidates, it's time to check the candidates' references. All questions of a reference check must be related to the job. It is illegal to ask questions of references that legally cannot be asked of the candidate (for example, age, race, sexual orientation, religion, creed, national origin, marital status, physical impairment or disability).

Do not contact any reference other than those provided by the candidate. Be consistent in the number and method of contacting references. Be sure to ask the same questions for all candidates.

Identify yourself immediately in your phone call, explain your position and tell the person why you are calling. Tell the person about the position for which the candidate is being considered. Start with general questions and follow with more specific questions such as:

- What are the candidate's strengths? Weaknesses?
- How did the candidate get along with his or her co-workers/supervisor?
- Was the candidate reliable?
- If appropriate, why did the candidate leave this job?
- Would you re-employ this candidate?
- Is there anything else that you would like to tell me?

Be sure to thank the reference for speaking with you.

The Hiring Decision

You have contacted references for every candidate whom you have interviewed and you have set your sights on one special candidate who has excellent skills, the essential traits and fine references. You are ready to extend an offer.

Call the candidate as soon as you are ready to extend an offer. The candidate may be interviewing for other jobs. This is a courtesy to the candidate and other employers.

After the candidate accepts the job offer, it is courteous to notify the other candidates that your vacancy has been filled. This can be done through a brief letter thanking them for their time and interest, advising them that the position has been filled and wishing them luck in their future endeavors.

A TARGETED APPROACH TO . . . SUPERVISION

Many years ago, a longtime member of my staff and her family lost their home in a fire. Everything in the house was gone, from basic needs to family heirlooms and precious photos. Before this incident, she had been the go-to person for all inexperienced staff. She was energetic and never asked more of anyone else than she did of herself. She paid attention to relationships, as well as regulations. I frequently delegated critical tasks to her, confident in her ability to capably execute them.

After the fire, however, things changed. She was distracted, exhausted and made mistakes. Given her circumstances, the entire staff was very spenly how the events in her personal life were affecting her professional life. She did not want to lose her job and I felt that we could agree on a course of action that would give her an opportunity to re-establish her once high level of competency.

We created a three-month plan of action to do just that. We agreed that I needed to supply more support and direction, as I had when she was a less experienced staff member. We would check in weekly to discuss her progress. For the next month, colleagues filled in for her at the morning program, giving her time to sleep, deal with insurance paperwork and purchase items needed to reclaim their family life. I took over her responsibilities for writing the monthly newsletter and managing the paperwork for the federal food program.

One month later she was ready to return to the duties of the morning program and was glad to increase her income that came with the additional hours of work. One month after that she was ready to resume writing the monthly newsletter and by the third month she resumed responsibility for the federal food program.

Over those three months, I spent more time by her side in the program giving positive feedback or redirecting behavior. She regained her personal strength and professional confidence. She showed gratitude to her colleagues for their support and eventually regained her leadership position in their eyes. This situation was a wake-up call to me that supervision is never stagnant. We created an intentional plan to move backward to preserve a valuable staff member and, over time, move forward.

Leadership & Supervision

Leadership isn't a one size-fits-all proposition. Effective leaders demonstrate a dynamic approach to hitting the mark — they adapt their skills to their followers' needs, providing the right balance between direction and encouragement to get the job done.

Leadership is meeting people where they are — and then taking them to where you need them to be. Leadership is the difference between telling someone to meet you along Interstate 70, which runs from coast to coast, and telling someone to meet you at Exit 27 on Interstate 70. If the supervisor knows precisely where you are on the route needed to travel, then she can reach you more quickly and engage you more effectively in the challenges the two of you face.

The concept is sometimes called follower-driven leadership. It puts the responsibility for building an effective team on the team leader by asking them to have a solid understanding of each person on their team and then adjusting their personal leadership style to fit the needs of each team member.

The Situational Leader by Dr. Paul Hersey (first published in 1984) is a classic text on this approach to leadership. Hersey uses a four-quadrant model as the basis for analyzing the follower's needs and the leader's response necessary to maximize results from the follower. The model is built in two dimensions with the horizontal axis representing the level of Task Behavior (or amount of specific direction given by the leader to the follower) and the vertical axis representing the level of Relationship Behavior (or amount of supportive interaction provided by the leader). The relative changes in these two characteristics generate four clearly defined quadrants that identify a follower's state of readiness to perform her duties and the best response by a leader in each of those situations to maximize the follower's chances for success.

Hersey labeled the quadrants as "telling," "selling," "participating" and "delegating." Generally speaking, a follower's movement through the model begins in the lower right-hand quadrant ("telling") where the leader is providing a high degree of direction and relatively low degree of relationship behaviors.

The follower then moves to the upper right-hand quadrant ("selling") where the leader provides high levels of direction and relationship behaviors as the focus shifts to more of a coaching role in response to the follower's need to understand why they are doing things in the specified manner. The upper left-hand quadrant ("participating") is where the follower progresses as she gains experience within her assigned duties and begins to gain confidence. At this level, the leader's response is to provide low levels of direction and high levels of relationship behaviors to nurture that growing confidence. Finally, the lower left-hand quadrant ("delegating") is where the follower has matured in her responsibilities to the point that she acts almost autonomously and is extremely self-motivated, resulting in relatively low levels of task and relationship behaviors by the leader whose role becomes more of a mentor.

SITUATIONAL LEADERSHIP®

One of the underlying principles in this leadership model is that it depends on the specific situation. That is, a follower can be a very skilled and confident performer in one set of duties — demonstrating all of the characteristics of someone in the "delegating" quadrant where their supervisor's input on task and supportive behavior is minimal — but that same person could quickly regress to a less capable state if, for example, new duties are added to her job description or a life-changing event occurs.

In that case, the supervisor would have to recognize that the follower's situation is now different and therefore the leadership style that is needed to help that person succeed must also be different. The leader may have to provide more direct guidance on the new job duties or vary the degree of supportive behaviors she offers until the follower is again confident and skilled in the demands of the new situation.

➤ See the chart on the following pages. A larger, printable version can be found on the CD-ROM included with this book.

This fluidity of response on the part of the leader is the essence of Hersey's Situational Leadership® model and a key for supervisors to effectively lead each member of their staff through a maze of changing responsibilities and assignments.

To meet the follower where they are in terms of performance, the leader must evaluate two determining factors — the follower's ability to do the job and their willingness to do the job. Hersey defines *ability* as "the knowledge, experience and skill an individual demonstrates in a particular task or activity;" while *willingness* is defined as having "confidence, commitment and motivation to accomplish a specific task or activity." The degree to which these two factors are present in a follower signals their readiness to successfully accomplish the assigned duties and suggests to the leader the proper leadership response that meets the follower's needs.

For a follower in the lowest readiness level — that is, someone who is unable to do the required task and is unwilling (or insecure) to do the task — the leader's best response is to apply a "telling" leadership style, providing a high degree of direction and lower degrees of relationship behaviors. A leader interacting with a follower who is at this level of readiness would provide detailed instructions on how, when, where and with whom a task is to be accomplished and then closely supervise the follower's

Quadrant 3: Participate

Team Member's Behaviors:
- First time "solo" performing task
- Lacks confidence and experience
- Needs feedback and encouragement
- Let me know if I'm on the right track
- Performance may be slipping — upset about things on or off the job

Supervisor's Response:
- Encourage team member's input
- Listen to the team member's concerns
- Allow team member to make important decisions
- Two-way communication and involvement
- Support appropriate risk-taking by the team member
- Celebrate successes; even small ones
- Explore and consider improvements and adjustments brought forward by team member
- Discuss possibilities and creative solutions

Quadrant 4: Delegate

Team Member's Behaviors:
- Consistently performs job to a high standard
- Operates autonomously
- Committed to and enjoys assigned task
- Keeps leader informed of progress
- Shares good and bad news
- Looks for ways to improve operations
- Proactive

Supervisor's Response:
- Delegate tasks
- Provide the big picture
- Treat like a partner
- Remove roadblocks so team member can accomplish more
- Share authority with team member
- Support the team member's decisions
- Appreciate the results
- Be available for team member (mentor)
- Inspire and motivate team member to excel

Quadrant 2: Sell

Team Member's Behaviors:
- Anxious or excited
- Interested
- Curious
- Some related knowledge or skill
- Receptive to input
- Engaged
- Enthusiastic

Supervisor's Response:
- Provide task-specific direction on who, what, when, where, how and why
- Take time to explain decisions
- Two-way dialogue
- Explain precise roles
- Allow team member to ask clarifying questions
- Invest time and training in the team member

Quadrant 1: Tell

Team Member's Behaviors:
- Intimidated by the job
- Unclear about directions she was given
- Feels like she is spinning her wheels
- Unclear about what's expected of her
- Frequently avoids responsibility or passes the buck
- She hopes a task will just go away
- Doesn't want to do the assigned tasks
- Thinks this job is a waste of time

Supervisor's Response:
- Make the team member's role clear
- Predominately one-way communication (from supervisor to team member)
- Hands-on help and training
- Incremental, step-by-step instruction
- KISS – keep it simple and specific

Note: Typical development shows a progression from Quadrants 1 through 4 but individuals may regress to lower quadrants as situations or responsibilities change.

performance. A follower who demonstrates this readiness level for other than brief learning periods, orientation or recovery from a setback outside the workplace is not likely to remain part of the team.

A follower who lacks ability but is motivated and making an effort is typical of a developing readiness level where the leader's best response is to demonstrate a "selling" style that offers the follower high degrees of direction and relationship behaviors. This is the traditional coaching mode where a leader continues to give direct instruction on the required tasks in order to establish the follower's skill sets while using one-on-one contact to help the follower understand the importance of why tasks are done a certain way. The leader wants to provide more insight and explanation to the follower on why decisions are made or specific tasks are required and allow for questions and clarification as the follower engages in these tasks.

The follower who is now able to do the assigned tasks but is either unwilling or insecure in doing them is someone who needs a "participating" leadership style from her supervisor. In this style, the leader does not need to give a high degree of task-specific instruction because the follower knows how to accomplish the work. However, she does need to build the follower's confidence by providing regular encouragement and motivation. The goal is to put the follower in situations where she can demonstrate her mastery of the required skills and thereby gain experience and confidence. Thus, the leader readily shares ideas with the follower and assists the follower's decision-making process. Confidence is the key component of this leadership response.

The final level of follower readiness is someone who is able to fulfill a task and motivated to do it. The follower has reached a level of self-confidence and self-motivation where the leader can now apply a "delegating" style that requires very little direction on task and very little relationship behaviors. The follower is acting autonomously in the assigned duties and has earned the leader's trust that the work is accomplished to the required standard. The leader can let the follower run with the ball. Developing a follower to this level is the goal of every leader because the benefit to the overall team is significant. These are valuable team members whose contributions and attitude elevate everyone's performance.

MAXIMIZING POTENTIAL

The concept of follower-driven leadership is one that offers the early-childhood or after-school professional a guide to maximizing the potential of her staff because it individualizes the leader's response to each team member and gives each the right amount of direction and support for the situation. It helps to avoid leadership miscues that frustrate a team or contribute to unnecessary turnover simply because the leader misunderstood what their team members required to be successful.

Consider, for example, the mature, highly motivated and skilled team member who is constantly being told what to do, how to do it and when by an overbearing supervisor. This micromanagement will eventually either diminish the high performer's motivation and performance or lead to her departure for a place of employment that recognizes and trusts her highly developed talents.

A similar leadership miscue but on the opposite end of the spectrum can be found when a new associate joins the team but is left to figure things out for herself without proper guidance and training. Leaders who are unwilling to invest the time to properly train and actively direct a new staff member's actions in the first few months of employment are setting that person up to fail.

Team members want to grow, learn, develop and succeed. No one takes a position expecting to fail but many do because their supervisor did not understand that leadership isn't telling the follower to figure it out or adjust to a one-size-fits-all leadership style.

Leaders who embrace a follower-driven leadership philosophy, who deepen their knowledge of Situational Leadership® and how it strengthens leader, follower and, ultimately, the team are leaders who can anticipate lower turnover of key staff members, higher productivity across the team and an energized work environment that is professionally stimulating and effective in the programs they create.

A TARGETED APPROACH TO . . . ORIENTATION

I was nervous and excited as I drove to the elementary school where I would spend my first day as the founding director of the after-school program. Upon arrival, I saw an available parking space right in front of the school. What luck! So I pulled in and parked.

About 20 minutes later I heard coming down the hallway, "Fe, fi, fo, fum! Who has parked in my parking space?" (Okay, maybe those weren't his exact words, but that's how it felt as he approached me.) This was, to my surprise, the principal of the elementary school and my new supervisor.

We had not yet met, as I was hired by the superintendent, but I felt certain that I was in the process of making a big first impression. And a bad first impression at that. This is how I realized that it stinks to have to get in trouble in order to find out what the rules are. It is much better to find out what the rules are up front, whenever possible. I vowed to try to do that for the members of the after-school staff and thus an orientation plan was born.

Orientation

Once a candidate has been offered and has accepted the position, an information packet is given to her before her first day. The goal of providing this information is to prevent your new staff member from getting in trouble as a way of learning the rules. This packet should include but is not limited to:

- a letter of introduction that welcomes the new staff member and describes proper work attire; expected arrival and departure time; the name of the person to whom they will report upon arrival; address of the program site and entrance door to use at the site; and any necessary transportation or parking information.
- a program handbook for staff members
- a program handbook for parents and families
- a program marketing brochure
- a description of their job and expected duties
- a time sheet

Also on that first day, take time to let your new staff member know how pleased you are that she is joining your team. Whether it is a sign on the front door on which you've written "Welcome," flowers, a piece of candy, a cup of coffee or a card, do something that sends a message that you have been expecting her and are delighted to welcome her as the newest member of this team.

Another important part of acclimating a new staff member is by making introductions to all key personnel. Have a checklist of everyone necessary to meet and check them off as you make each introduction. It is easy to miss someone because she is out of her office or classroom. The checklist will help you to remember those who still need to be introduced.

A tour of the program site is a great way to orient a new member of the staff. It provides plenty of visual aides to help the employee learn about the program. No detail is too small on the tour. Files that are filled with registration and parent contact information, allergy and medical issues, photo release forms, weekly program planning sheets and much more, need to be discussed. Cabinets that contain supplies, equipment and materials need to be explored. Hand-washing procedures need to be modeled and taught. Combinations for locks need to be memorized. Activity resources need to be reviewed so they can be used when planning programming. And this is just the beginning.

A common occurrence during this comprehensive site tour is to see a glazed look cross over the face of the new staff member. She may continue to nod her head as if receiving information. However, the glazed look is a telltale sign that no more information is actually entering her brain.

To combat this, implement a scavenger hunt for all new staff members. Start by creating a list of everything you want staff members to be able to find in the program. Be comprehensive. For example, ask them to find the location of the construction paper or where snacks are stored or the telephone number for the program. Give new staff members two weeks to scavenge around the program and hunt for or learn about everything that is on the checklist.

Encourage them to ask anyone for assistance. This serves as a way to help new and experienced employees to bond. Once they fill in the blanks, it is their reference sheet for finding or knowing everything essential about the program. This kind of experience gets the glazed look off their faces and helps them to become more comfortable with using materials and taking action in the program. You can also add to the scavenger hunt the names of key personnel whom you want them to know. List their roles and have the new employees fill in the blanks.

Another necessity for orientation is thoroughly discussing the job description and expectations. Provide concrete examples and give plenty of opportunity for answering questions. Whenever possible, use scrapbooks, videos or photos as visual aids to help illustrate the job responsibilities.

Review the parent handbook and the employee handbook to make sure that all policies are clearly understood. Have new staff members sign and date a form that states that they read, understood and will follow all policies and procedures detailed in the handbooks.

Also, on every new employee's first day, coordinate a date, time and location for a one-on-one meeting in 30 days. It is important to schedule this on their first day because, even with the best of intentions to make individual time for staff members, time slips away. Explain that, at this time, she will be expected to review her strengths and challenges.

THE FIRST WEEK

It is not unusual for a new employee to start her career as an early-childhood or after-school professional by being given a group of children and a pat on the back. This must change.

There are certainly challenges to providing time for training and orientation when your program is out of licensing compliance with the staff-to-child ratio, but it is not appropriate to send a new staff member into a classroom without proper training. It is actually the perfect setup for constant staff turnover when proper training and orientation are lacking. It also sets up new employees for getting in trouble trying to find out about the rules.

To prevent this, allow new staff members to spend the first week on the job without direct responsibility of a group of children. Instead, they can spend that week observing and shadowing co-workers; getting to know the children and families; learning how to plan activities; familiarizing themselves with resources, materials and equipment; integrating understanding of program policies and procedures; meeting key personnel; and going through introductory training. Imagine the capabilities and confidence of this new staff member versus one who walked in and tried to figure things out as she went along. There is no comparison.

THE 30-DAY REVIEW

The 30-day review is an extension of the orientation process. This is an opportunity for staff members to ask questions about their job.

Ask the new employee to discuss her strengths or the contributions that she has made to the program in the first 30 days. Then ask her to discuss any struggles or challenges she is facing. The conversation could be a great deal shorter if a director describes only the strengths and challenges that she has observed. Instead, this exercise gives the director an opportunity to see how self-aware the staff member is.

Sometimes new staff members can be harder on themselves than a supervisor would be. In this case, point out contributions that she may not realize she is making to the program.

On the other hand, some new staff members can be blind to their poor habits and behaviors. This is an opportunity to bring those to light and to work on improvements. More times then not, new staff members are fully aware of the strengths and challenges. This is a chance to acknowledge how clearly they see themselves.

A TARGETED APPROACH TO...
BUILDING RELATIONSHIPS

My first day as the director of an after-school program was when I was fresh faced, wildly enthusiastic and straight out of college. I was sharing space with a kindergarten teacher who did not share my level of enthusiasm for the program location. I chose to focus on the children and how to make their first day in the after-school program one to remember. Upon their arrival, they unanimously chose to play outside. The children and I exited through the kindergarten classroom door and I heard it close with a resounding thud.

I didn't think much about it until the children were sweaty, thirsty and ready to go inside. It was then that I discovered that the thud had been the sound of the door locking firmly behind us. I reassured the children that it was nothing to worry about and then proceeded to go door by door, trying to get into the school. All the doors were locked. I looked up at a second floor window and spied the custodian. Without hesitation, I jumped up and down and screamed at the top of my lungs, trying to get his attention and assistance. No response. I reached in my pocket and found my car keys. At this point, I had nothing to lose, so I unlocked my car, laid on the horn, and got his attention (as well as several neighbors and a stray cat).

The custodian, whose name I did not yet know, opened the door without a word. However, as he rolled his eyes, turned on his heals and walked away, I clearly felt his disdain. I just didn't understand why. What had I done? That thought kept me awake that night.

It began to occur to me that in my excitement to establish the program, I had focused on the needs of the children and families that the program would serve. I put my energy into planning creative learning opportunities, choosing healthy snacks and writing policies and procedures. What I had not done was recognize how these activities, snacks and policies were going to impact the lives of a kindergarten teacher and a custodian. They had not been consulted or included in any of the decision-making about the addition of the after-school program.

It was time for me to figure out ways to show appreciation and build positive relationships, not just with them but with the other employees at the school. In doing so, I also needed to show them how these are "our children" — not "their children" during the school day and "those children" after school, to which I so often heard them referred.

We have common goals that we can achieve through communicating our needs and cooperating along the path. Whether it's improving literacy skills or preventing childhood obesity, we can be partners.

The bridge to building a better relationship with the custodian, Clarence, started by introducing myself to him and finding out a little about him. Among the things I learned was that his birthday was coming up in two weeks. This gave me an idea.

The children and I spent time during the next few weeks preparing a surprise party for Clarence, complete with homemade gifts, cards, wrapping paper and a small cake that we made in a toaster over. After luring him to the kindergarten classroom, he was greeted with shouts of "Surprise!" and the singing of "Happy Birthday." He was shocked and once again speechless, only this time his body language conveyed appreciation and warmth.

This began an ongoing streak of good deeds where we decorated Clarence's cleaning supply closet with streamers, balloons and notes of appreciation. An extra snack was made available to him daily. He was invited to all of the children's performances and more. In return, our program had paper towels, toilet paper and soap as needed. We were welcome in the gym after school because Clarence changed his cleaning schedule to accommodate the children's need for large motor skill activities in inclement weather. We talked openly and frequently. But most important, we become partners in doing what was best on the children's behalf.

Having learned a valuable lesson, we then tried to build positive relationships and to show appreciation to all school leaders on an ongoing basis. Like all relationships, they require attention, clear communication and willingness to give and take.

....
Building a Team That Hits the Mark

Building Relationships

New staff members tend to shy away from introducing themselves to parents and family members. Don't give them that option. Those introductions are critical to developing positive relationships between the staff and families. Make sure, for the sake of safety and relationship building, that there is a staff member assigned to be the greeter at every morning and/or evening program.

Even though staff members are supervising children, short conversations and friendly comments with their family members can go a long way to developing trusted relationships. Then, should the need arise to discuss problems that a child is having, there is a foundation of trust established.

To assist families further in making a connection with a new staff member, place her photo and biographical information by the sign-in/sign-out sheet so families can get to know a bit about the newest person in their child's life. If you have a newsletter, bulletin board or Web site, also post it there.

Coaching

Orientation is a major component in getting any new staff member off to a successful start in the early-childhood and after-school fields. But to truly create an early-childhood or after-school professional, it's crucial to provide coaching to staff members of all levels.

For example, provide opportunities for experienced staff members to practice their leadership skills by having them mentor or coach new employees in their first few months. Put in writing the responsibilities of the mentor or coach and make sure that she is ready to take on this role.

This can help forge relationships between existing and new staff members. It is often more comfortable for new employees to ask questions of a peer than of a supervisor. This does not relieve the supervisor of any responsibilities. It is a method of reinforcing the support for new staff members as they begin their employment.

It is during this ongoing coaching that the assessments made during the 30-day evaluation become a valuable tool for the director, staff member and program.

Review the evaluation and discuss ways to transform what had been identified as challenges into goals for improvement.

This process is the Professional Growth Plan. The Professional Growth Plan is a process by which to establish a culture of positive reinforcement for guidance and growth of individual staff members.

Professional Growth Plan

The first step in the plan is to state the goal. This can be done by reviewing the challenges that were noted in the 30-day evaluation. Select one to focus on as the employee's goal. Often there is a desire to tackle more than one. However, it is better for new staff members to start simply and have success then to overload them and experience failure.

State the goal in positive terms, such as: *To better understand the developmental needs of fourth- and fifth-graders and plan appropriate activities with them.* A goal is something positive you are working toward. A challenge is something negative that you are fighting against. Therefore, transforming the challenge to a goal changes the energy in a direction of positive resolve.

The next step is to define the strategies that aid the staff member in meeting the goal. Are any tools needed, such as books, videos, one-on-one mentoring or training or a class or college course? Would an opportunity to shadow an experienced staff member or a site visit to another after-school program assist in the process? Discuss ways that this new staff member learns most effectively and select strategies that will likely work for her.

➤ An example of the Professional Growth Plan is on Page 77. A printable version can be found on the CD-ROM included with this book.

Even though two members of the staff may be working on similar goals, their strategies to reaching them may not be the same because of their different learning styles. Write the goal in a positive manner and be specific such as:

• *Read* Real World Connections *and focus on ideas for working with fourth- and fifth-graders in after-school programs.*

• *Attend the Programming for Older School-Age Children training sponsored by the local Child Care Resource and Referral agency on Sept. 14ᵗʰ.*

• *On Sept. 20ᵗʰ, shadow and observe Jane Smith's techniques for working with the fourth- and fifth-graders.*

Next, be specific and clear about the resources that will need to

BUILDING RELATIONSHIPS

be gathered or arrangements that will need to be made for training, shadowing or mentoring to take place. Using the previous example, the resources needed to meet the established goal are:

• *A copy of* Real World Connections.

• *A registration form from the local Child Care Resource and Referral agency for Programming for Older School-Age Children and the funds to pay for it.*

• *Request that Jane Smith, an experienced member of the staff, who has a gift for working with fourth- and fifth-graders, spend time with the new employee. Additionally, a substitute will be needed to cover for the new staff member while the shadowing and observation takes place.*

Using experienced staff members for shadowing, mentoring and one-on-one training can be very effective. As the supervisor, you have been observing this new staff member. Be clear with the experienced staff member regarding what you want them to emphasize in their training.

Also be clear and specific with the new staff member when stating her responsibilities for meeting this goal. In this example it might be:

• *Read* Real World Connections *and implement ideas on working with fourth- and fifth-graders in after-school programs.*

• *Attend training on Programming for Older School-Age Children and implement ideas learned.*

• *Shadow and observe Jane Smith's techniques for working with fourth- and fifth-graders and implement ideas learned.*

The Professional Growth Plan allows for success because the supervisor states specifically what she will do to assist her new staff member to reach her goal. There are times when staff members fail because they do not get the support, resources or supervision that they need. By stating the supervisor's responsibilities, it holds her accountable for her actions as well.

For directors who are supervising multiple staff members, this is a way to provide individual attention in a focused manner and with a clear timeline for responsibilities. In our example, the supervisor's responsibilities might be:

• *Give a copy of* Real World Connections *to the new staff member and instruct her to pay special attention to the section on working with fourth- and fifth-graders.*

• *Register the staff member and pay for the training on Programming for Older School-Age Children. Provide the staff member with the location, date and time of training and with any necessary paperwork. Make clear your expectations of what the employee should get from this experience.*

• *Make arrangements with Jane Smith for the shadowing and observation to take place. Additionally, arrange for a substitute to cover for the new staff member during this time. Be clear with Jane and the new staff member your expectations for this experience.*

The most subjective part of the plan is establishing a timeline for the employee to meet the goal. The timeline will vary from one staff member to another because of different learning styles, experience, education and personalities. The intensity of the goal will affect the length of time required to achieve it, too. Using the above example, four weeks would be the recommended time needed to read the book, attend the training, shadow the colleague and implement the ideas that were learned. It is important to continue to observe and support the new staff member as she implements changes in an attempt to meet this goal.

Establishing a date, time and location for reviewing progress and setting new goals allows the new staff member an opportunity to ask questions and get clarification. It is a time to celebrate strengths and to discuss challenges that have taken place during this process. You can expect one of three things to have happened:

• THE STAFF MEMBER WILL HAVE ACHIEVED HER GOAL. *With this staff member we celebrate. Then the Professional Growth Plan is started again with yet another goal. It may be a challenge that was identified previously or it could be something new that one of you has discovered needs improvement. The process is identical. Only the goal has changed.*

• THE STAFF MEMBER HAS PARTIALLY MET THE GOAL BUT NEEDS MORE TIME OR DIFFERENT STRATEGIES TO REACH IT. *Her attitude is positive as supervisor and employee attempt to make changes and improvements. Thus, the supervisor gives her the additional time needed to reach her goal or changes the strategies to be more suitable for her learning style. A new timeline is established for achieving the goal and reviewing progress. Supervision and support is provided to help her to be successful. Once the goal is reached, the process begins again with a new goal.*

• THE STAFF MEMBER HAS NOT SHOWN AN EARNEST ATTEMPT TO LEARN AND MAKE IMPROVEMENTS. *Her work ethic and attitude reflect someone who is just going through the motions. An open discussion is had about why she has not reached the goal. If she is willing to change her attitude and work ethic then another chance is given. However, the timeline for achieving the goal is shortened and the supervisor will need to see that a genuine effort is being made to improve and implement changes. At the next meeting, if there is little change, than a discussion regarding more suitable employment will take place. This process provides documentation that may be needed for the termination of this employment. If the goal is achieved and the attitude has improved than a new goal is established.*

The Professional Growth Plan is a process that is repeated on an ongoing basis with each member of the early-childhood or after-school staff. It is a way to nurture individual growth in each employee. It holds the supervisor and the staff members accountable for contributing positively to professional growth and program improvement.

Professional Growth Program

Targeted goal

Strategies to meet the goal

Resources needed to meet the goal

Staff responsibilities

Supervisor's responsibilities

Timeline for meeting

Date, time and location of next meeting to check progress

Sign and date the PGP

A TARGETED APPROACH TO . . .
MOTIVATION

Many years ago, I visited S&S Worldwide, a century-old, family-run company in Colchester, Connecticut. They employ several hundred people who manufacture and distribute materials around the globe for craft kits, therapy, physical education and the early-learning field.

Yet when I arrived in the lobby that day there was a big sign that read, "Welcome Tracey Ballas, CEO of School-Age NOTES. We are delighted to have you here!" I was blown away by the personal touch and thoughtful gesture.

Upon touring the facility and meeting the employees, it became evident that this sign was representative of the corporate culture that S&S Worldwide created. To this day, whenever, I see the S&S Worldwide logo, catalog or booth, it puts a smile on my face.

Their act of kindness influenced me to re-examine the methods I use to motivate my staff. As a leader, I became more determined to model appreciation and to establish this as an important part of our program culture. I was more intentional about frequent, simple actions that showed gratitude toward individual staff members and the team as a whole. By modeling this behavior, it became contagious and staff members began showing more appreciation toward each other.

After increasing my efforts to provide staff motivation to my staff members, the results were tangible. Staff members' satisfaction and performance were markedly improved. It became a place where people enjoyed coming to work and making a difference instead of just a place where they put in their time and received a paycheck.

Motivation

One of a leader's fundamental responsibilities is to motivate her team, and for good reason. Teams that are motivated are more productive, experience less turnover, demonstrate greater creativity and are better able to handle change. Workplaces where motivation is part of the culture project a more appealing image, express a more optimistic environment and generally feel less stressful.

In *Super Motivation*, author Dean Spitzer points out that 50 percent of employees put just enough effort into their work to keep their job. That means half of your organization is working at the lowest possible levels of productivity and effectiveness. Injecting clear, consistent and sustained motivation into the workplace can encourage the half that is withholding their full efforts to step up and contribute more to the team's success.

This is a point worth emphasizing: Fully half of an organization's workforce is performing at a level just above what it would take to have them fired. That means they are capable of delivering more on the job than they are showing; a lot more. Even an organization's best performers are still likely holding back skills, ideas, energy or effort that they could be expending in their job but aren't. That reserve is called discretionary effort and it is the mother lode of performance riches to leaders who can tap into it.

By focusing on motivating an employee to unleash that discretionary effort, a leader can rapidly improve the overall productivity, effectiveness and morale of almost any team. Motivation is the key that unlocks that differential and turns potential contribution into actual results.

Motivation is not complicated and can start with something as simple as appreciation. According to O.C. Tanner, a company specializing in organizational recognition programs, "Appreciation is acknowledgment of a job well done. It can be expressed in many ways, but when used effectively, it changes everything. It awakens talent. Inspires creativity. And cultivates possibility. Appreciation starts small. A note to say thanks for working late. Movie tickets for going the extra mile. But when nourished, appreciation grows into solutions that change the culture of your workplace and move the company forward."

Appreciation goes hand-in-hand with recognition; the two concepts complement each other. But there is another reason leaders should be appreciative of their people — turnover. Research shows that 79 percent of employees cite lack of appreciation as a reason for quitting their jobs. And turnover costs money.

Leaders sometimes lose sight of the extraordinary costs that an organization incurs every time it has to replace someone. There are obvious costs such as advertising, interviewing and, if needed, moving a new employee. These are just the tip of the iceberg. Every search takes leaders away from their primary job. The loss in productivity is substantial for tasks such as considering what skill sets are needed in the replacement, where to advertise, reviewing resumes, interviewing and screening candidates, checking references and additional productivity lost by adding others to the interviewing process.

As an example, the cost to replace one management person at Cornell University's campus life division just a few years ago cost about $24,000. Reducing turnover rates can save the organization substantial expenses in time and resources, so an investment in motivating your team can pay real dividends.

Motivation is not cheerleading. It's not about imploring the team to perform at a high level but inspiring them to do so. Motivation requires the leader's engagement, focus and commitment. One of the best ways to motivate your team — and the absolute cheapest way — is to be visible and active in the workplace. People don't want their leaders behind some desk or locked in an office. Being out and interacting with your team, seeing what they see, dealing with what they deal with, being part of the day's performance, means a lot to most people.

This stems from a leadership principle that reminds leaders that they should not make their absence from the workplace a reward for good performance. The philosophy runs counter to some perceptions that say, "The less I see of my boss, the better." Adhering to that negative approach is demotivating. Good leaders are inspiring. They help their team. They put to use their experience and ideas so their team can excel. You want good leaders around — they are motivating just by being there.

If recognition is what you do to lift your team, then motivation is how you do these things. Motivation is an attitude and a language. It's about caring enough about your team to set the bar high and giving increasing levels of responsibility and challenge. It's knowing your team well, evaluating strengths and weaknesses, potential and pitfalls, successes and setbacks. Motivation communicates constantly. It rarely assumes and never takes for granted. You see recognition but you feel motivation.

A TARGETED APPROACH TO ...
RETENTION

At the beginning of each school year, unbeknownst to my staff members, I would send a letter to each parent who had a child enrolled in our program. I would express to them how talented and hard-working the staff members were. Their children, of course, were the beneficiaries.

I would ask for their help in gathering donations for gift certificates or small gifts of appreciation that would be given to employees for a job well done throughout the year. I asked them to tap into any accessible resources among family, friends or their workplace.

The response was overwhelming. Each year I would receive movie and theater tickets, gift cards for sporting goods, restaurants and salon and spa treatments. Stuffed animals and candy, bath oils and lotions were donated.

Families, even those on a tight budget, recognized that Monday through Friday, they counted on these professionals to be caring, dependable, safety-conscience, creative, important influences on their children's lives. They generously helped me build an arsenal of gifts to say thank you to these underappreciated professionals.

Before I sent this letter, this phenomenon of thankfulness never occurred. Parents weren't unappreciative, but sending this letter stimulated awareness among them about the role this team plays in their lives. We also established a culture of gratitude between the families and the staff members.

Staff members who are shown recognition and appreciation are motivated. However, retention comes when they feel valued and are given opportunities for meaningful involvement. In addition, they feel empowered from working in an environment that provides opportunities for professional growth and development. This is a formula for staff retention. It is also why regular staff meetings and training are so central to retaining a team that you have worked so hard to build.

Retention

Numerous studies have shown that it costs less money to train and retain an employee than to continually train new employees. While having vacancies from time to time is a reality, creating a work environment that is pleasant and rewarding will result in a workplace where employees want to stay.

Use staff meetings as an opportunity to foster the idea that you want your employees to grow in their jobs. This lets them know that you have confidence in them and helps them have confidence in themselves. Good staff meetings are intended to provide opportunities to learn, exchange ideas, share information, solve problems and create unity. It is not meant to be a time for complaining, venting or making power grabs.

There is a direct link between the type and quality of spatial environments and the stress that staff members experience. Where the organization of materials and space are at odds with needs of the staff, frustration accumulates, dissatisfaction intensifies and poor performance results, writes Paula Jorde Bloome in *Avoiding Burnout*. Although she may have been referring to program space, it is no less true regarding meeting and training space.

STAFF MEETINGS AND TRAINING THAT FOSTER RETENTION

There are many things to consider in creating a conducive environment for having staff meetings and training sessions.

Get things off to a good start by greeting team members by name as they arrive. Exude positive energy. It is contagious. For new groups, set ground rules for expected behavior such as the use of cell phones or text messaging during meetings. Write these down for the group to see and adhere to them at all gatherings. Make sure that you have turned off your own cell phone.

Be professional and respectful by starting on time and ending on time. As the person leading the meeting or training, refuse to be interrupted, unless it is an emergency.

Have materials such as the agenda, handouts and resources organized to save time and keep the team focused. If using a DVD player or giving a PowerPoint presentation, test the equipment ahead of time to make sure there are no technical glitches.

Get team members talking and engaged right away. Use ice breakers, brain teasers and games as tools to create unity. But select them with the intention of illustrating a point or to introduce information that you want to share with the group.

Offer praise in meaningful ways at staff meetings and trainings. Find out what motivates your team. Public acknowledgements? Token gifts? Awards or certificates? This does not replace one-on-one feedback with individual staff members but rather is a way to include appreciation and gratitude in the team culture.

If it is a long meeting or training, schedule appropriate breaks.

Give staff members an opportunity to contribute to the meeting agenda in advance. Once the agenda is developed and the meeting begins, stick to the agenda. At the beginning of training sessions, clarify the goals and objectives that will be covered.

Let staff members evaluate meetings and training sessions as a means of feedback about what they learned, what more they need to know and how supervisors can improve the delivery or process.

Check the meeting space in advance for proper setup, comfortable temperature and ventilation and good lighting.

Be a role model of tasteful humor, good grammar, punctuation and enunciation.

Consider other ways to set the tone or create a positive atmosphere by using tablecloths, playing music as team members arrive, having refreshments available or incorporating door prizes.

To lower stress and show consideration, avoid having meetings and trainings during particularly busy times of the year.

If the team is working on an ongoing project or training, clarify the next steps before the group disbands.

Close meetings and trainings on a positive note. Consider inspirational stories, poems, music or a closing activity.

Additionally, encourage staff members to join professional organizations at the local, state and national levels so they can attend conferences, have access to professional journals and newsletters and network with fellow professionals. If your organization or program can afford to pay for membership for staff members, do so. This provides an opportunity to work with other professionals and unite with others for child advocacy and for worthy wages. (Consider joining the Worthy Wage Campaign — www.ccw.org/index.php?option=com_content &task=view&id=24&Itemid=53). Subscribe to professional magazines and newsletters that are made available to staff members. This stimulates awareness of issues in the field, offers creative programming ideas and encourages professional development.

When selecting topics for training, consider the areas that need to be strengthened in individual staff members, as well as the team.

If your team is made up of Conductors, Connectors and Cruise Directors, then each individual brings to the team specific skills that you desired at the time that you hired them. While a Conductor remains detail-oriented and organized, she might be in need of some training to help strengthen her relationship-building skills. The Connector has those relationship skills mastered but might need some training in creative program planning. The Cruise Director may have a bounty of creative ideas but needs some help in getting organized. Target training to help each member of the staff to strengthen her weakest traits or skills.

There are so many factors that make the early-childhood and after-school fields challenging career choices. The positions are often inadequately compensated, part time and without benefits. Yet few professionals have as much impact on the lives of children and families.

➤ For a list of potential topics for staff training, see Page 78. A printable version can be found on the CD-ROM included with this book.

According to the National Center for the Child Care Workforce, the presence of a consistent caregiver who is sensitive, well-trained and well-paid correlates to high-quality child care. Therefore, intentional efforts need to be made to retain staff members for the well-being of children and the peace of mind of families. It can't be something that a leader does on occasion as an afterthought. Regular time and creativity need to be devoted to meaningful ways to retain staff.

Try to create full-time positions. Many programs are matching staff members up with other positions inside their agency or in neighboring agencies to be able to offer full-time work.

Provide the best possible wages that your program can afford. As stated previously, it is more cost-effective to invest in salaries than frequently hiring new employees because of staff turnover.

Impress upon your employees the importance of raising awareness about staffing shortages and salary issues to families, employers and legislators. This can be done through a program newsletter, letters to the editor to your newspaper, or public speaking engagements. Let families know when staff members leave for economic reasons. Discuss these issues at parent and family meetings to help them understand the scope of the problem. It may motivate them to assist with fundraising events, make donations to the program, volunteer or advocate for worthy wages.

A TARGETED APPROACH TO . . .
EVALUATION

In the course of conducting trainings, I often ask participants what events have helped them to grow as leaders. One woman told a story that, unfortunately, was identifiable to several in the group.

According to the woman, a supervisor would criticize staff members publicly, creating an environment in which all of the employees would visibly freeze as the supervisor approached. During a 90-day evaluation, the woman brought this up to the supervisor, explaining that while she appreciated being told when she wasn't doing something right, she said that being corrected in front of her colleagues was unpleasant. In addition, she asked if there couldn't be a little positive reinforcement, too.

The supervisor told her that correcting her in front of others allowed everybody to learn from everybody's mistakes and that she didn't believe in providing positive reinforcement, because what does anybody learn from that? This woman told her supervisor that what she and all of her colleagues were learning was that they didn't like working in that environment. Not surprisingly, turnover was high.

The woman in the group said that experience has stayed with her and now, as a program director herself, she makes a concerted effort to mention positive observations of staff members in evaluations and makes a point to compliment staff members in the presence of colleagues.

Evaluation

Regularly evaluating employees and providing them face-to-face feedback on how they are doing, where they are going and how you (their supervisor) can help them get there are among the most important responsibilities a leader has. It is essential to building the kind of team that excels in their work and stays motivated through challenging times. Like motivation, evaluation — or rather, the lack of serious evaluation — is one of the primary reasons employees leave an organization.

The traditional view is that people leave for more money. In fact, according to a Saratoga Institute survey of nearly 20,000 exit interviews, 89 percent of employers believe that people who voluntarily leave the organization do so for more money. The actual number of employees who leave for more money is 12 percent. The disparity highlights the delusion leaders cling to believing that employees mostly leave for better pay rather than recognize the fact that far more leave for reasons more personal and avoidable. People don't leave jobs, they leave supervisors.

In that same survey, "lack of career growth and advancement opportunities; no perceivable career path," was the second most cited reason for an employee leaving, following poor management in importance to people who chose to move on. Imagine that for a moment: The second most significant reason driving voluntary turnover is that the employee did not see her future there because no one communicated it to her. Good employees leave when no one notices they are there and when no one communicates to them what they can accomplish. They stay not because they see a paycheck but because they see a future.

That is why leaders must make it a priority to conduct regular evaluations that include honest, direct performance feedback, show a path of professional development and outline a road map on career growth.

How regularly should you provide this type of formal evaluation? The answer to that can vary from quarterly to twice a year but no less than annually. Your team needs to know what that schedule is and that you will adhere to it. Few things are as demoralizing as anticipating a performance evaluation that never comes because everything else causes it to be postponed. What message does that convey to the employee? Speaking with you about your performance is obviously not as important to the leader as the latest crisis, or at least that is what the employee perceives. As a leader, set an evaluation calendar and stick to it.

There are as many evaluation systems as there are leaders to think up one and no one is inherently superior to the other. The first critical factor in any evaluation system is that it honestly assesses the employee's job performance over the period measured and in the agreed-to areas of responsibility. It needs to be written down with each point of the evaluation discussed in a closed-door, uninterrupted setting that allows the leader to explain her assessment and the employee to respond. Praise and constructive criticism should be present in any evaluation — a balance that should be communicated upfront so the employee can anticipate feedback on both.

The second critical factor is to identify the areas of greatest need in order to correct sub-par behavior or to advance skills that show even greater potential in the employee. Limit these to no more than three areas, if possible, as creating a laundry list of to-do items generally results in unfocused efforts coming out of the evaluation and eventual frustration.

The third critical factor in any evaluation system is a road map that discusses the next steps in job growth, skills development and career path. This is where the leader helps the employee to see their role evolving within the organization; visualizing the employee taking on new challenges or responsibilities; aspiring to a leadership position or expanding in their current capacity. Evaluations that only look backward rob the employee of an opportunity to grow and that often contributes to their undesired and unanticipated departure.

One evaluation system that can be adopted easily calls for an annual written performance appraisal supplemented by a formal mid-year progress meeting. Both meetings are documented in writing with the employee taking a copy and a copy being added to her personnel file. Typically, the annual appraisal includes all three of the critical factors outlined while the mid-year progress meeting focuses less on the long-term career goals and more on the short-term performance measurements associated with her core duties. Allow one hour for the annual performance appraisal meeting and 30 minutes for the formal mid-year progress meeting.

It is important to take steps to ensure that there are no interruptions during the time you meet. Both people should silence their cell phones. The leader should put her office phone on "do not disturb" and a closed office door should suggest that only an emergency would trigger an interruption. This creates an environment in which the leader and employee can have a guided dialogue (where the leader guides the time and topics).

Start the session on a positive note if possible. Welcome the employee and thank her for her continued contributions to the team. Remind her that this is an important part of her employment and that you value this opportunity to share with her your observations about her performance and potential. Tell her that it is essential that you share areas of praise and areas of opportunity and that she should expect to hear both from you. Let her know that there may be areas of disagreement and that is all right but that in the end this is a document that reflects your perceptions and expectations of her work and so the two you may have to agree to disagree on some points.

Follow that with a big picture view of her job as you see it, touching on a few key responsibilities and what you look for from her in her current capacity. From there, move into specifics about her job performance taken directly from the completed appraisal document. Be as specific as possible. Use examples that illustrate your opinion or observation. Speak to the results or impact of the employee behavior and your level of satisfaction. After each major point, let the employee respond.

Listen intently and do not interrupt but remember that evaluations are not intended to be debate sessions. You are not negotiating your appraisal of her performance, you are conveying it. If a particular point is more contentious and you need to keep the meeting on track or on time, then tell the employee that you appreciate her passion on the issue and you will be glad to set up a follow-up meeting to focus just on your differences on that issue.

Once you have covered the core responsibilities within the employee's job, turn your attention to possible professional development goals or training you might recommend for her. Most employees welcome opportunities to learn, grow or expand their skills so every good evaluation should include planning for a future professional development experience.

Close the document review portion of the evaluation session by covering what you see as a career path or job growth for the employee. Speak optimistically about the employee's future and her ability to reach these new goals. You want the employee to visualize the new opportunities to grow within your team and sense your commitment to helping her achieve those new heights.

An effective evaluation session is the product of hours of good preparation on the leader's part. Give yourself time to fully and accurately complete the performance appraisal document so that its content is meaningful and relevant to the employee. This is not something you toss together on a whim or that you delegate to the employee to complete on her own. This needs to be one of your core responsibilities as a leader; one of those duties you make time to do right.

The few hours you invest in constructing a comprehensive evaluation and giving that appraisal to the employee pales in comparison to the weeks you would spend if you had to replace one of those good employees who chose to leave because she saw no career growth or advancement opportunities. Take time to get this right. Your organization can't afford to lose good people because you were too busy to tell them how valuable they are!

A TARGETED APPROACH TO...
TERMINATION

Early in my human-resources career, there was a period when I found myself involved in a string of employee terminations. The issues varied but what was common to each was my distaste for the meetings themselves. I just didn't like terminating people.

In the wake of that series of terminations, my boss — and mentor — shared with me an observation that has come to define my attitude toward ending someone's employment: "When it stops being difficult is when it's time to do something else."

That simple thought helped me realize that while letting someone go is one of the least pleasant aspects of leadership, showing compassion and consideration for an employee can make the process a little more bearable for everyone involved.

Termination

By following the guidelines and suggestions in this book, you will create a template for hiring the right people for your program. But there will come a time when you will have to let an employee go.

When viewed inside the context of the employment life cycle, termination becomes just another responsibility that leaders must execute to maintain a healthy, vibrant and productive program for the children. It is not a responsibility that leaders enjoy, but one that confronts every leader. As such, it is an aspect of leadership that needs to be understood and respected.

It is important to realize that termination — except in the most extreme or egregious circumstances — is the end of a long trail of events that has unfolded over time.

➤ For a sample termination letter, see Page 79.

Employee reductions based on decreased operating revenue or loss of funding or similar economic downturns are an unfortunate but not uncommon state of affairs. But these are benign circumstances that do not elicit the same consternation for program leaders that the process of firing someone for cause brings. But if the employment life cycle process has been managed correctly, no one should ever be surprised that she is being fired.

The most common situation that leaders encounter is an employee whose performance is not acceptable. The deficiencies could be any number or combination of factors — unreliable attendance, ineffective interaction with the children, inability to work as a team with colleagues, inappropriate temperament or communication styles, insubordination, laziness or other violations of organizational policies, procedures or standards. Whatever the reasons, the termination process begins with the recognition that an employee's behavior has not met your expectations and needs well-documented corrective action.

The "well-documented" aspect cannot be overemphasized. Every stage of the termination process leading up to separating an employee requires a paper trail. This series of corrective-action notices documents that the employee is made aware of the problem, given guidance on what is needed to correct the problem and an acceptable timeframe to make those changes, and that the employee understands that continued deficiency jeopardizes her employment. The supervisor and employee should sign any corrective-action document with the employee receiving a copy and the original going into the employee's personnel file.

This corrective-action document serves several purposes. The first is that it helps the leader organize her thoughts on what the specific deficiencies are and what changes are necessary to correct the problem. Second, it emphasizes for the employee the seriousness of the issue and alerts her to the possibility that her job is in jeopardy if the problem is not corrected. Finally, it serves as a legal foundation to justify the termination action should the matter be challenged later in court.

Any written notice of corrective action before termination should contain some common information:

1. The employee's name and the supervisor's name

2. The date that the meeting to discuss the corrective action was held and who was present for the meeting.

3. A description of the deficient behavior or performance including date(s) the behavior or performance was noted, specifics about the incident(s) and the result of the deficiencies.

4. An action plan detailing changes in behavior or performance that are required including any remedial training (and who will provide that training).

5. A timeline to accompany the action plan outlining the date(s) of remedial training, scheduled progress meetings and a not-later-than date to have all deficiencies addressed.

6. A clear statement of the consequences of failing to adhere to the action plan and the timeline, and how to correct the behavior.

7. The employee's and supervisor's signatures (Note: The employee's signature indicates that she has had the content of the disciplinary notice presented to her and she understands what is expected to correct the deficiencies and the consequences of not doing so.)

8. One signed copy for the employee to take and the signed original copy for the employee's personnel record. (Note: The termination notice is usually a letter signed by the supervisor and does not ask for the employee's signature)

Unless you are governed by a collective bargaining agreement, there is no standard process that dictates how a supervisor must proceed in a disciplinary progression. Common steps include a verbal warning, which is also documented in writing; a written warning; a suspension (often three days without pay); and finally, termination. This particular process allows the employee three opportunities to correct the deficient behavior before she is terminated and documents repeated attempts by the supervisor to gain compliance and satisfactory performance from the employee.

Of course, the severity of the deficiency is a major consideration in the length of the process. There are obviously extremely severe incidents of insubordination, dishonesty, abusive behavior, etc., that cannot be tolerated and would require no progressive discipline. But short of these extremes, the supervisor must determine the severity of the problem, the likelihood it can be corrected, the method of intervention and the timeline for restoring acceptable behavior or performance. The multistep disciplinary process works well when performance adjustments need to be made or when policy/procedure infractions (such as attendance, inappropriate language, etc.) are the issue.

As part of an employee's personnel record, these documents may be subject to use in legal proceedings related to the termination so care should be taken in preparing them. It is also a good idea to have your documents reviewed by legal counsel before terminating an employee.

Terminating an employee is serious and must be done with the utmost professionalism and respect. It is an action that is necessary at times but one best handled privately and quickly. The meeting should be in an office where the door can be closed. The supervisor should have a second manager present (the assistant program director, for example) to verify that the meeting is conducted professionally. Often, the end of the day and/or the end of the week is a good time for the termination meeting to minimize difficult interactions with colleagues afterward. Termination meetings are not long or involved, perhaps 10 to 15 minutes.

The supervisor and second manager should be in place when the employee is called into the office and the door closed. Small talk should be avoided as the meeting needs to quickly take on a serious tone. Once the parties are seated, the supervisor should lead the discussion indicating that this is a difficult meeting for everyone. The supervisor should then briefly detail the circumstances justifying the termination, including failure to make acceptable progress on corrective action surrounding deficient performance or an explanation of the egregious act that triggered the termination.

The supervisor can offer the employee an opportunity to briefly reply in case of an extraordinary rationale that might mitigate the termination decision (a very rare instance), but in the absence of compelling evidence to alter the decision the supervisor should advise the employee that she is terminated, present her with the termination notice and ask for keys, badges or other critical employment items she may have been issued. Assuming the person is composed, the second manager should accompany the employee to her workstation to retrieve any personal items and then ensure that she exits the building promptly. This needs to be done with tact, but is important to ensure that no incidents occur.

The meeting could sound something like this. Supervisor Terry and assistant program director William ask to see Francis.

Terry: Francis, come in, please. William, will you close the door. Francis, this is a difficult meeting for all of us. Unfortunately, we have not seen the progress in your performance the past month that we had anticipated. You will recall that we met with you a month ago regarding your tone and mannerism when interacting with the children. We provided additional training twice in the past four weeks aimed at helping you improve those skills but unfortunately we have not seen the necessary improvement in that area. This latest incident on the playground yesterday reinforced the fact that you have not been able to alter your behavior. I'm afraid that there is not a place for you on this team now and today will be your last day with the program."

Francis: Terry, you know I've been trying to apply what you've taught me but yesterday was just a lot of little things frustrating me and I let that frustration out by yelling at some of the boys who were rowdy. I shouldn't have done that but I don't want to lose my job over it. Can't we extend my warnings one more time?

Terry: Francis, I appreciate that you recognize your behavior was not appropriate yesterday but it was just one of several times we have observed or had reports of your conduct not meeting our standards. I'm sorry but this is my decision. Here is a copy of your termination letter — I will need you to leave your building keys and ID badge with me. William will go with you to your workstation and help you retrieve your personal belongings. Again, I know this is difficult for all of us and regret that things ended here the way they did. Good luck.

CONCLUSION

The rewards for the leader who can successfully build and balance a team of professionals are significant and far-reaching. They benefit the leader who now has a high-performing team she can rely on to accomplish challenging goals. They benefit the team that can enjoy a workplace where synergy is the norm and staff is allowed to develop fully. But most of all, they benefit the children who are the reason that the early-childhood or after-school program exists in the first place. Engaged children thriving in a dynamic learning environment are the product of a well-balanced team of talented professionals committed to their work and to continuous improvement.

This book is intended as a resource for leaders in the early-childhood and after-school fields to use in their own professional development and to build high-performing teams. To that end, it may be helpful to revisit one of the critical insights in this book regarding hiring the right team members. Specifically, it is worth pointing out a tendency many leaders have to over-rely on the strength of a team member's skills instead of the quality of her traits. It is not uncommon to have a blind spot when valuing traits. Skills are easier for us to recognize, validate and sharpen so we have a penchant for adding (or developing) team members based on skill level. Traits are harder to identify and more stubborn to change but they are also the tiebreaker that ultimately determines a team's effectiveness.

Traits feed team chemistry, so they can be worth the extra time it takes to reveal them in an interview or to observe them in a probationary period. When interviewing, screen for skills but hire for traits.

That is, use skills as the measurement to reduce a candidate pool to a final few. Paring down a large number of applicants based on skills ensures that the necessary tools to perform the work are there. But use traits as a way to zero in on the final selection. Skills tell you where a person is at that moment; traits suggest where it is they have the potential to go.

Remember that skills can be mastered and traits can be mustered but in the end, leadership in any field is about continuously sharpening the former and valuing the latter. The challenge is to know how to balance that in your team and in yourself.

Leaders have to hit the mark every time they step into the workplace. Thus, leaders must not only lead with confidence, but also train those they hire to lead, too. It is the true leader who recognizes that by passing her skills on to others she is creating a team that delivers targeted leadership for her program, the children and their families.

Keep this in mind every day as you aim high, strive to be your best and hit your mark!

RESOURCES

- Terms of Endearment
- Where to look for staff members and volunteers
- Sample telephone interview questions
- Professional Growth Plan
- Potential topics for staff training
- Sample termination letter

Terms of Endearment: A starter set

General

being flexible
being professional
being a problem solver
being punctual
being reliable
being self-motivated
being energetic
being responsible
being tolerant
being a team player
being honest
being trustworthy
being accountable
being self-aware
being a good
    communicator
being ethical
being mature
being proactive
being open-minde
being friendly
being principled,
    dedicated,
    committed
    and fair
being eager
being observant
showing initiativ
showing common sense
modeling good hygiene
modeling a positive
    attitude
coming to work for
    more than the pay
    check
having an appropriate
    sense of humor
possessing experience

Conductor

organized
detail-oriented
prompt
computer-literate
good writer
accounting back-
    ground
good follow-through
punctual
neat
orderly
careful
well prepared
has a plan B
reliable
multitask oriented
flexible
aware of rules,
    regulations,
    procedures
safety conscience
a problem solver
efficient
diligent

Connector

nurturing
loving
kind
caring
child-centered
warm
compassionate
friendly
sociable
collaborator
gentle
good listener
amicable
good communicator
positive attitude
considerate
empathetic
sympathetic
big hearted
concerned
patient
team player
good at networking
relationship builder
people-oriented

Cruise Director

fun
resourceful
vibrant
creative
energetic
artistic
playful
active
musical
athletic
imaginative
ingenious
multitask-
    oriented
organized
well prepared
flexible
charismatic
outgoing
inventive
lively
good planner
optimistic
innovative
vital
enthusiastic
dynamic

Where to look for staff members and volunteers

- **Community colleges and universities:** Recruit students pursuing degrees in early-childhood education, child development, elementary education, social services or related fields. Also consider students studying to become a professional in recreation, art, drama, music, computer technology or any area that will benefit your program. Professors, teaching assistants and department leaders also may be able to recommend potential candidates.
- **Child Care Resource and Referral Agencies:** locate local resource and referral agencies at www.childcarerr.org.
- **Professional organizations at the local, state or national level:** Check out their Web sites to see if they have a job posting board. Attend their conferences or trainings and network with the intention of meeting and recruiting quality staff members. Spread the word among colleagues.
- **Employment agencies online and those with local offices**
- **Religious communities:** Ask if the church, synagogue or mosque has a regular newsletter, bulletin board or a Web site where job openings can be posted. Also, find out if they would be willing and able to announce the opening at services, meetings or events.
- **Community service organizations and clubs:** Contact groups such as the Kiwanis, Lions and Rotary Club. Research if they also have a local Web site or newsletter for posting job openings. If not, ask if an announcement can be made at their regular meeting time.
- **Principals:** If your program is located in a school, speak with classroom teachers, guidance counselors, music teachers, art teachers, coaches, student aides, parents, etc., regarding potential staff members.
- **Families of children currently enrolled in your program:** They have a vested interest in who is caring for their children and often have good contacts.
- **Your staff members:** They have vested interest in who is hired to be their colleague.
- **Consider volunteers to enhance and add richness to your program:** These unpaid members of the staff can help improve the quality of your program. However, if you have a licensed program, volunteers cannot be counted in the staff-to-child ratio. Volunteers will need training to make sure that they are providing quality care

that is consistent with your policies and procedures.

Some resources to consider for recruiting volunteers:

• **RSVP:** The Retired Senior Volunteer Program connects volunteers who are 55 and older with service opportunities in their community. Go to www.seniorcorps.org/about/programs/rsvp. asp or call 202-606-5000.

• **Americorp:** A network of local, state and national programs that connects more than 70,000 Americans each year in intensive service in education, public safety, health and the environment. Go to www.americorp.gov or call 202-606-5000.

• **High school and college students**

• **Grandparents of children who are enrolled in the program**

RESOURCES

Sample Telephone Interview Questions

What is one decision in the course of your professional experience that you consider a mistake and what would you do differently if you had the chance?_____

_____

Which is more important, fair and consistent policy administration or a passion for creating excellence in children's programs?

_____

_____

What is one example where you considered yourself a coach/mentor to a colleague? _____

_____

What is one example of a time you worked one-on-one with a child to guide them through a challenging situation or circumstance?

_____

_____

What characteristics describe the supervisor you are most motivated to work for? _____

_____

Describe your ideal work environment. _____

_____

What salary requirements do you have and where are you currently? _____

_____

May I contact your references? _____

Professional Growth Plan[1]

State the goal: _____

Strategies to meet the goal: _____

Resources needed to meet the goal: _____

Staff's responsibilities: _____

Supervisor's responsibilities: _____

Timeline for meeting the goal: _____

Date, time and location of next meeting to review progress and set
new goals: _____

Signed and dated by staff and supervisor

_____   _____
(Supervisor's signature)   (Employee's signature)

_____   _____
(date)   (date)

[1]Adapted from Strategic Problem Solving by Cathy Heenan

Potential Topics for Staff Training

- Goals/mission/philosophy of program
- History of organization/program
- Funding of program
- Understanding who we serve in this program
- Personnel policies and procedures
- Program policies and procedures
- Meeting the developmental and individual needs of children and youth
- Guiding behavior
- First aid and CPR
- Prevention of child abuse and neglect
- Emergency procedures and fire safety
- Daily schedule and program management
- Creating partnerships with families, schools and community
- Designing quality indoor and outdoor environments
- Planning and implementing developmentally appropriate activities
- Safety, health and nutrition
- Professionalism
- Working with children and families with special needs
- Embracing diversity
- How to be an advocate for children
- Good communication skills
- How to observe children and assess program quality
- Resources available for program planning and support

Sample Termination Letter

(Letterhead)

(Date)

(Name)

This letter is formal notification that your employment with (organization) is terminated effective today, (date). This letter is presented to you in a meeting attended by myself and (name).

I appreciate your service and many contributions to our organization but I have concluded that your continued employment is not aligned with our needs or expectations.

To assist in your transition, I am authorizing two weeks of paid severance. Accrued vacation, holiday or other financial benefits to which you are entitled will be paid accordingly. Your coverage under our group health and insurance plan(s), including any standard employee deductions, will continue at the employee rate for the two-week period of your severance. COBRA benefits, as provided for by law, will be extended thereafter.

It is necessary to immediately return any and all keys, cards, business records or other items relating to your employment that may be in your possession, including passwords to any business-related software.

It is always a difficult decision to separate an employee but I believe that the current arrangement does not meet the needs of the organization. Our policy on employment references is to verify dates of employment and position(s) held.

I wish you well in future endeavors.

Sincerely,

REFERENCES

Branham, L. (2005). *The 7 hidden reasons employees leave.* New York: AMACOM.

Herrigel, E. (1999). *Zen in the art of archery.* New York: Vintage.

Hersey, P. (1992). *The situational leader, 4th ed.* Escondido, CA: Center for Leadership Studies.

Jorde Bloom, P. (1989). *Avoiding burnout. Strategies of managing time, space, and people in early childhood education.* Lake Forest, IL: New Horizons Books.

Making work pay in the child care industry: Promising practices for improving compensation. (1997). Washington, D.C.: Center for the Child Care Workforce.

O'Connor, S. (2002). *Reducing turnover: Strategies and models for programs and communities.* [Handout]. Wellesley, MA: National Institute on Out-of-School Time at the Wellesley Centers for Women.

Pike, R. (1989). *Creative training techniques handbook.* 130-135. Amherst, MA: HRD Press Inc.

Trieshman, A., Whittaker, J.K., & Brendtro, L.K. (1971). *The other 23 hours: Child-care work with emotionally disturbed children in a therapeutic milieu.* Chicago: Aldine Publishing Company.

Whitebook, M., Bellm, D. *Taking on turnover. An action guide for child care center teachers and directors.* (1999). Washington, D.C.: Center for the Child Care Workforce.

ACKNOWLEDGMENTS

A special thank you to Ellen Gannett, director of the National Institute on Out-of-School Time, for believing in me when I was just a pup. I am so fortunate that you saw in me untapped potential and skillfully drew it out. Thank you for being my teacher and mentor, and for exemplifying leadership.

I also want to thank Ruth Fitzpatrick, the former coordinator of School-Age Care for the Kentucky Department of Education. You are the essence of persistence, boundless energy, creative problem-solving and innovative thinking. You challenged and stretched me in ways that have changed my life.

I owe a debt of gratitude to Kathy Hermes for her loyalty, generosity and dependability. You have been my sidekick in fulfilling so many professional dreams, from starting the National AfterSchool Association to developing the School-Age NOTES Foundation. You made the smallest detail look effortless and gave me permission to create the big picture. I am so blessed to have you by my side.

To the late Rich Scofield, my friend, colleague and mentor, I miss you every day!

To Marci Press, ever the cheerleader, thank you for believing in me. You gave me strength and encouragement every step of the way. How lucky I am to call you my friend!

Much of what I know is thanks to the uplifting, soul-filling, idea-fueling colleagues and mentors who have dramatically influenced my professional growth. I cherish the diverse ways that they have enriched my life. I am deeply grateful to Dale Boreman Fink, Jill Bradley, Ellen Clippinger, Renee DeBerry, Ana DeHoyos-O'Connor, Molly McNally Dunn, Bettie Gehring, Diane M. Genco, Elizabeth Joye, Martha Krall, Susan O'Connor, Marc Robinson, Michelle Seligson and Dawne Sterling.

Additionally, I would like to thank Diane Barber, Diane Bennett, Patty Cole, Sandy Davin, Barbara Dubovich, Coleen

Dyrud, Janet Frieling, Kathy Haugh, Judy Goldfarb, Cathy Heenan, Joan Lombardi, Judy Nee, Roger Neugebauer, Roberta Newman, Mari Offenbecher, Curtis Peace Jr., Flo Reinmuth, Peggy Riehl, Leslie Roesler, Steve Rosen, Linda Sisson, Darci Smith, Judy Tough, Yasmina Vinci and Paul Young.

If you want to write a book, here's what I recommend: Find yourself an Erika Konowalow. She is the person who will meticulously and lovingly read, edit and improve every element. It is easy to trust her because she exudes experience, talent, good judgment and a sense of humor every step of the way. Next, place the manuscript in the hands of a creative wonder like Key Metts, who can flawlessly lay out and design the words in a way that makes this book a pleasure to read. This dynamic duo has brought these pages to life and I am so grateful for their combined talents.

ABOUT THE AUTHORS

TRACEY BALLAS is the chief executive of School-Age NOTES Inc., (www.schoolagenotes.com) and the founder of the School-Age NOTES Foundation (www.schoolagenotesfoundation.org). She is also an education and training associate for the National Institute on Out-of-School Time (NIOST) at the Wellesley Centers for Women.

Ballas was one of the founders of the National AfterSchool Association, serving as president for six years. She also was one of the founders and past president of the Ohio After-School Association.

After many years of running programs in early-childhood centers, public schools, churches and YMCAs, Ballas became the statewide coordinator of both the Ohio Child Care Resource and Referral Association and the Ohio Project on Out-of-School Time.

She has testified in Congress and served as an advisor to former Vice President Al Gore on the Welfare to Work Committee. She has been featured in articles for *Child*, *Working Mother*, *Parenting* and *Child Care Exchange* magazines.

With nearly 25 years invested in the early-childhood and after-school fields, Ballas brings a wealth of experience and passion to the keynotes, workshops and trainings she has conducted throughout the United States and Europe. Her expertise extends to programs large or small, single or multi-site, for-profit or not-for-profit, military or civilian.

To bring Tracey to your next event, please contact her at:

School-Age NOTES	Phone: 614-296-7209
P.O. Box 476	E-mail: inbiz4kids@aol.com
New Albany, OH 43054	Web site: www.schoolagenotes.com

 **CHRISTOPHER NOVAK** is a professional speaker who has inspired thousands of people nationally and internationally with his "Conquering Adversity" message. Based on his first book, this powerful, true-life presentation focuses on the hero inside each of us and what it takes to rise above change, challenge and adversity in our professional and personal lives.

Novak is also the author of two leadership development books, *4 Circles of Good Business* (Core Concepts, Inc., 2006) and *Lead Like a Pirate* (Cornerstone Leadership Institute, 2007) and more than two dozen articles in publications that include *HR Magazine, Newsweek, Smithsonian's Air & Space* and *CUPA-HR Journal.*

Novak is a seasoned human resources executive who has held senior-level positions with Cornell University and Syracuse China Company. In 2001, he started his own professional development company, The Summit Team, focusing on leadership training and executive coaching.

He has a bachelor's degree in aeronautics-mathematics from Miami University of Ohio and a master's degree in business management from the State University of New York.

To bring Chris to your next event, please contact him at:

The Summit Team	Phone: (315) 673-1323
P.O. Box 172	E-mail: info@summit-team.com
Marcellus, NY 13108	

Web site: www.ConqueringAdversity-speaker.com

INDEX

If you enjoyed this book, consider purchasing others published by School-Age NOTES.

School-Age NOTES is a proven provider of practical resources in areas such as:
• administration & training
• tools for trainers
• creating environments
• enrichment
• fitness & games
• summer

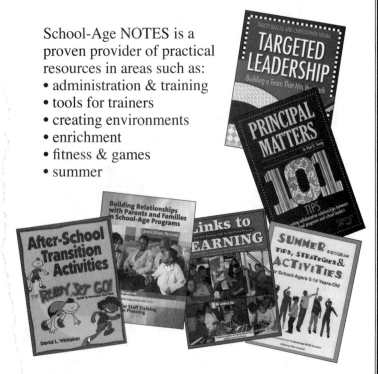

Tracey Ballas, owner of School-Age NOTES, is available to speak on such topics as:
  • leadership   • building relationships
  • social contracts • training new staff members
To book Ballas for training, or speak with her about creating a workshop specifically for your program, call her at 614-296-7209 or send an e-mail to inbiz4kids@aol.com.

School-Age
NOTES
Resources for AfterSchool Professionals